Life is so beautiful

Life of a girl

MJ

ISBN 978-93-5610-739-7

Published in India 2022 by Pencil

A brand of
One Point Six Technologies Pvt. Ltd.
123, Building J2, Shram Seva Premises,
Wadala Truck Terminal, Wadala (E)
Mumbai 400037, Maharashtra, INDIA
E connect@thepencilapp.com
W www.thepencilapp.com

CONTENTS

Foreword

Hlo I am MJ nice to meet you all ....

I am from India .... This is my life story.... We all know Indian culture god and lifestyle....

Their is a lot of temple mosque gurudwara in India .... Also ae trust in that statue who is made by us and human

. We give food to them . We give milk oil rupees to them but we didn't think about that poor people and children who even don't have 2 rupees to eat something...the statue didn't say any word from

his mouth that give me this ......the god is not in them .....open your beautiful eyes and see where is real god ...in statue or in poor....

We light candles in church but if we give candles to poor so we don't do any wrong things ......

We pray from god ....that give me lot of money i take fast for you

If the pray is accepted by taking fast then the poor is having owner of millions......

Preface

The story starts from girl house . She is an Indian girl . When she was 10 . She is very kindness girl. She always

Think about others. She is from middle class family

but happy family . All things goes

Properly but one day her father comes and she saw taht her father drinked first time . The time goes continuously her father always drink ed at night with his friends and comes home late.

She has 2 sister s and 2 brother. Her big brother is disable. She born after 2sister and small brother is after her . Her name is Rani .

After 6 years later

Her family condition is now.......

Her father beats her mother at night. Karma said " if a man expects a woman to be an angel in his life. Firstly create heaven for her . Angels don't live in hell.

But in her life .

In school she always smile in front of her friends but inside she lost in her problems.

She has a best friend. Her best friend said always to her that say everyone that you are 4 brother and sister her best friend feel guilty because her best friend is having a disable brother.

When she is in 9 class. They divide the class in 9A and 9B . She is in 9B and her best friend is in 9 B .

Her life is changed now.......

She meet a lot of friends who take care of her. One boy who always flirt with girls

And he also flirt with her. One day she bunk the class. She studying

But also live and enjoy the life with that bastard friends . Also her class teacher doudt that a boy is her boyfriend but she didn't know that he is only Rani's friend.

But now in her family they not fear with her father. One day at night her father comes late at home . And her father drinked a lot that's why he can't ride thd bike and slipped in the seaver . Some boys going from that way so they help of her father

They bring him to his home. The grandfather angry too much . Her father comes inside the house. Her grandfather said to them thanks a lot. The boys goes from there. Her grandfather comes inside the house and take slipper and beats in her father cheeks .

Rani's mother stop to her grandfather . Her grandfather also abusing to her father a lot. She said nothing. She puts all talks in her heart .

When she was 15years old......

In summer vacation she go in her village with her 1sister and grandfather, grandmother. A boy in the village who loves her . He proposed to her and she don't having any feelings for him but she asked to her sister;"if I said to him no ...so what happened..."his sister said;" he don't feel good and get to much sad...."

Then she said,"if I said yes to him then ...."his sister said,"he is too happy..." She don't take care of her feelings. She said yes to him and he do from Village to his town and she also go her town

The summer vacation is over.

Her sister search his I'd and she talk to him in I'd . After few days she see that he always come online but he didn't reply and response to her. He always give late reply to her . She breakup with him by her heart . And she never talk to him .

The flirty boy alway said to her i love you but she ignore him .

In class 9 she met a new girl who live in same place. She made her friend and her friend is having a boyfriend . We all know that in adult age we having a attachment to any person .

She and her friend go to in her boyfriend place to buy milk. Her boyfriend having many friends and she also talkna lot with that boy . She thinks that she loved with him

But she didn't know that this feeling is called attachment. Then she comes in relation.

1month later she knew that this is only an attachment because her sister

also tell her attachment with a boy that she gave the name of love . So that's why she also breakup with him.

In class 10th now her real love story begin from here .....

The flirty boy always said her i love you but she didn't response to him . He always

come near to her and sit with her . All class teasing to them .

He also hold her hand .

But now the feeling comes for flirty boy by her. When she saw him and he came closer to her the heart beat continuously. She don't know what the feeling comes in her heart when she saw her. But one day that boy made a girlfriend who study in her class . She didn't show jealousy in face but she jealous . They sit together and hold each other hands .

But one day she talk the boy in WhatsApp. They talk a lot . He said

to her can u come in relationship with me .

She said but you are in relationship .

He said but I love you not her . Then a message comes to her from her friend

She see that her friend write s that Rani, please said yes to him ..he really loved you....

Her friend continuously message to her and he also .

Then she said yes to her .

They got too much happy ,he call to her and they talk too much.

She thinks that he only loved her .

He said to her when she breakup with me then I come with u..

She said ok.

After 2-3 days he didn't break up with her . He said that she won't break up with me

She said it's ok I move back and I didn't come in the middle of you and her . He said sorry'.....

She breaks a lot with her family issues and one more breaks her heart .

After 2-3 month later ...

He and she got break up. He said that she too much jealous when I sit and talk with any girl .

Then he asked to her can u come in relationship with me. She said no and I didn't come in relationship with any one now. There friendship is like that some days thay talk a lot and somedays they act like that they didn't know each other . They are like stranger.

The COVID -19 comes in India. The lockdown is start and their talks is stopped.

After 8 months later the schools are opens . They go to school.

Rani and he didn't talk to each other but after some time they talk a lot . But

again COVID comes so lock down is start.

In lockdown her family condition.....

Her father drink a lot . Her disable brother got fever. His health is not well . His body is like skull

The grand father, father takes care of the brother a lot but medicine didn't work.

In 8 June 2021 morning...

Her brother Died in front of all family members . Now she didn't believe in god . For *her*

The god is died because she pray for her brother a lot . But the god didn't listen her prey

But one day at evening the TV opens the "Mahabharata " comes . She didn't want to see but her soul

Push her to see Mahabharata . She see that Krishna said to Arjun ," no one can live permanently in world one day that live this world . This is the rule of the world ."

When she listens that thing. She thinks a lot . She also think at night. Then she realised that death is the bitter truth of this world. Now

She believes in kanhaji a lot .

After some days her father drinked. In the school the fees is pending a lot of her and her brother and sister. The school stuff said to them always that submit your fees but they don't have money.

One day her father is having a accident. Her father hurt in his mouth but hurt too much.

Her father take to much loan from many people the people comesIn her home to take money.

After few months later her father is very sick her mother take too loan for her father

Now she knew that a wife can bring back her husband's life even from the mouth of death ..... Her mother takes care a lot of her father and she also . Her father get well.

After few months later the school is open. Her big sister vis in the college and her 2sister having board exam so her fees is submit by taking loan . Rani is not good at study . She like to write story , k drama made paintings,anime . She is in class 11 and she failed in 1 subject so she gave retest and pass the class . Now she is in class 12. She just wants to do something for her family. Too many times her father break her heart because he said that he didn't trust in her , you can't do anything in your life bla bla.....

Now she live the life with her break heart.....

This is the story of Rani....

Life quotes

∆• when the darkness knock the door so the happiness is hide somewhere and we want to find our happiness in the darkness their is a hope with us and that hope is kanhaji.....

∆• Women are better at love than men

That's why god made the mother.......

∆• Live your life With your own method not others methods...

Δ• Little by little , day by day what is meant by you it will find a way.....

Δ• whatever happened, happened for good, whatever is happening, happening is good , whatever will happens,

Will also happens the good

Δ• if you don't fight for what you want Don't cry for what you lost....

Δ• love is most beautiful thing in the world that can't be seen, can't be touched, it can only be

Felt in the heart....

Δ•if you do not get your love than definitely give love to those

Who love you .....

Δ• funny have some times a person who is thousand of miles away from you can make

you feel good than people right next to you.......

Δ• And a solution to all your problems is Krishna ....

Δ• seeing some one's pain if you also have pain then understand that Krishna

Is seated in your soul......

Δ• love is that condition in which happiness of another person is essential to your

One.......

Δ• some times your heart needs more time to accept

What your mind already knows......

Δ• He said, where there is love , there is my grace...."

Krishna

Δ• To love without condition, to talk without intention,

To give reason and to give without expectation that's the spirit of soul......

Δ• how many obstacles were seen in love ,

Still saw Radha with Krishna.....

Δ• Krishna's love is like an ocean you can see it's beginning but the beautiful thing is that

You can't see it's end......

Δ• if you think he is not answering your prayers.

Just remember , he feels your pain ......

Δ• Krishna knows what you want and

He will give you what's best for you.......

Δ• nothing is constant in this world every grief and sorrow

Comes to teach the lesson of life ....

Δ• It is better to live your own destiny

Imperfectly than

To live imitation of some body

else'slife with perfection...........

Δ• if you want to know what will happen to you in the future look

At what your mind is doing now

KARMA......

Δ• you learn more from failure than from success

Don't let it stop you failure builds

Character.........

Δ• two things I'll forever be sure of the sun will always fall for

Moon and I will always fall for you

Krishna..........

Δ• keep Krishna in the centre of your life and do everything for him

This is real dharma.......

Δ• if you fail to achieve your goal Change the strategy!!!

Not the goal.......

∆• other may arise doudts over your ability and effort but if you do

Not believe in your self,

This is the same confessions of your failure.........

∆•earn two friends in your life

One like Krishna who will not fight but will make sure you win......

And another like Karna who will fight for you even when you are wrong.........

∆• never touch a women ego !!!

One day she may burst

Life a volcano.........

∆• what parents do for us

And what they get in return......

∆• Freedom comes with sacrifice....

Δ• never underestimate the importance of small steps

Δ• one day you fell Life is difficult,

But then the results can be very great ....

Δ• always remember that you are an influence

In some body life.....

Δ• Don't be sad if someone reject you

People usually reject expensive things and go for cheaper ones......

Δ• love is based on respect not

Face cut and body shapes........

Δ• sometimes you don't even realise what god

is doing for you.........

Δ• only mother can sacrifice and smile both at same time......

Δ• when you approach with love

Krishna reciprocate with love.......

Δ• the body has many needs

But the soul has only one to be with Krishna.........

Δ• Krishna is real soulmate of every soul.........

Δ• everyone talks about a mother's love

But never see a father's sacrifice........

Δ• use the pain as fuel and keep going.......

Δ• some people sell happiness while

They don't taste any for it.........

Δ• before you build for others

Build your own castle first.......

Δ• a good book can change your life........

Δ• never wish life were easier,

Wish that you were better.........

Δ• Happiness is a state of mind........

Δ• LIFE is not same for everyone.......

Δ• no one is coming to save you ,

Your life is 100% your responsibility......

Δ• when love is true ,

Then even deadlist become loveliest........

Δ•How you see the world depends on how you look...........

Δ• only true friend stab you in front..........

Δ• nowadays people are forced to wear a fake smile...........

Δ• stop creating problems that aren't even there ....

Δ• Never ever depends on anyone if they leave you will get broken severely.........

Δ• nobody on earth can ever love you more than your parents.......

Δ• don't expect victory without a fight ....

Δ• the best way to help yourself is to help someone else...........

¶• don't judge others you are not perfect..........

Δ• some people poor by money but rich by heart'.........

Δ• believe in yourself........

Δ• when you overthink everything you end up hurting yourself.......

Δ• life is like a boomerang you get back what you give.......

Δ• we meet everyone for a reason either they are a blessing or a lesson.......

Δ• spirituality is not about for god truth or the ultimate,

But about learning to just look.......

Δ• Love is that condition in which the happiness of another person is essential to your own ......

Δ• the closer i I get the more I see from far I am.........

Δ• patience is when you're supposed to be mad but you choose to understand........

Δ• TO those who have conquered themselves,

The will is a friend. But it is the enemy of those who have not found the self within them........

Δ• Krishna is the most beautiful name in the world.......

Δ• darkness Can't drive out darkness only light and do that hate can't drive it

hate only love can do that.......

Δ• when you turn your worry into worship

Krishna will true your battles into blessing......

Δ• the struggle in life is not time management it's priority management.......

Δ• why do you worry without cause?

Whom do you fear without reason?

Who can kill you?

The soul is neither born nor does it die ....

Δ• we come in this world empty handed........

Δ• the world is perishable and whenever comes to this world surely has to go one day

Δ• truly can never be destroyed,

One should not be afraid of doing good.......

Δ• what have you lost that you cry for ?

What did you bring that you have lost ?

What did you create that was destroyed?

What you have taken that has been from here ?

What you gave has been given here?

Δ• what belongs to you today belonged to someone else's yesterday and

Will be someone else's tomorrow ....

Δ• change is the law of universe ....

∆• Radha Krishna love is very precious

Explain to the whole world the value of love ....

∆• if you like someone you will hold him

And if you love him you will free him ....

∆• do everything you have to do

But not with ego not with lust not with envy

But with love compassion humility and devotion........

∆• it is better than beating the head at the door is fate

Creating a storm of deeds

The door will open automatically

∆• 3 reason why you should smile every day

God loves you

God listen you

God always be with you

Δ• life is not qualified by fluent English branded clothes or a rich lifestyle

It is measured by the no. Of faces who smile when they hear your name......

Δ• if you don't have the right word for a situation then just smile

The can get entangled but smile always work........

Δ• the colour blue represent his infinite force . He is bluish because he is infinite, cosmie and

Immeasurable like the sky which end cant be discovered.......

Δ• I have purpose for your pain

A reason for your struggle and

A reward for your faithfulness

Trust me and Don't give up

Δ• Change is the law of the world

In a moment you become the owner of millions

And in other you become penniless......

Δ• have faith in God's grace

There wherever you go, you will achieve victory .....

Δ• stop counting two things in your life

Your own sorrow and other happiness....

Δ•The relationship of love can broken by saying a lie

But the relationship of heart can never be broken...

Δ• cheating is a choice,

Not a mistake...

Loyalty is a responsibility not a choice

Δ• waiting is a sign of true love and patience

Anyone can say I love you but not everyone can wait and prove it true's....

Δ• you can become very dangerous when you' ll learn how to control your feelings and emotions. ....

Δ• people make the mistake of choosing the wrong person first and when the right person arrives they just stop trusting people ....

Δ• trust his words

Trust his decision

Trust his vision

Trust his deeds

Trust kanhaji once, he entrust himself forever.....

Δ• smiling has always been easier than explaining why you are sad

Δ• god end's anything on a negative

God always ends in positive....

Δ• I am true believer in karma

You get what you give whether it is good or bad ...

Δ• the world gonna judge you no matter what you do so live the life the way you want to...

Δ• if you focus on hurts you will continue to suffer

If you focus on the lesson you will continue to grow....

Δ• the only women who understands me is my mom.....

Δ• life is a book everyday a new page every month is a new chapter and every year is a new series......

Δ• death is not the greatest loss in life

The greatest loss is what dies inside us while we live

Δ• death is bitter truth of life

Δ• don't tell your secret to anyone your today's bestie is your tommorrow is worst enemy....

Δ• don't be too happy when people say they love you and care you

The real question is until when!

Because just like seasons people change

Δ• if you' ll prioritize chanting

Krishna will prioritize you

Δ• if it's true

It will stay

Δ• Krishna is not punishing you. He is preparing you .

Trust his plans not your pain

Δ• and then there's some conversations that you just save for the god

It's because only god provide the kind of comfort that humans cannot

Δ• These black clouds in the sky reminds me of my fears and

I love it when it rains on now well it hide my tears

Δ• fear is not an obstacles

It's an illusion because fear is only made by you

Δ• if you want to be strong learn to fight alone

The second story is of a animal or a boy .....

The story starts from the boy house. The boy name is Raj.

He sleep in his room and a box open and a dog come out of that box and tried to pick him up by licking

His mouth. He wakes up and brushes his tooth . His mother call him ," Raj come on for breakfast..." Raj said," ya.. I am coming". He wears his school dress and come to kitchen for breakfast. He say ," good morning..mom" and sit in his seat and doing breakfast. His father comes and sit for breakfast. Raj said," good morning....papa

His father said," good morning......I want to ask you that you didn't take that dog again. " Raj said," no ...no..."

His father said," don't tell a lie if you bring that dirty dog so it is my last warning get out that dirty dog...." Raj said," please papa I can't do this with shiro" his father said," if you can't do this so I can "

Raj caught his father legs and requested from him .but he didn't listen to him

go in his room. The shiro sleep in his bed . He wake Up and licking him but he is in so anger he catch him so badly and throw him out from the house . Shiro get hurt too much

His father warn to everyone....and go to office.

Raj crying in his room. Raj's mother said to her," mummy Mahesh...." Her mother said," i know all things"

Then she go in Raj room . He is crying their. She put hand on his head . She strocked his head . She said," i know my son that why are you crying.... You think about shiro .." her grandma support him and give love to him.....

Then he go to school. He meet with his friends who know all things about his family....When school is over

Raj go in ground to meet shiro . He bandaged him and give him food . And said ," their is no one who understands me accept you...."

At night the rain come suddenly . He think about shiro

So he go IN ground shiro is wet in rain he made a house for shiro.

And give him food...

Then he go to house.....

Next morning he is I'll and he can't go to school ... Her grandma come and said," don't worry i give food to shiro ....ok...""

He is too happy and hug grandma..... laugh

Two days later.....

Her Grandma have a heart attack ..... suddenly...they admitted her grandma

But her grandma has died he cry too much ....

5 YRs later

HE Made a big business man . But shiro has get lost somewhere.

He search him every where but he didn't meet him.....

But suddenly one day

In night time he see that a girl who is having shiro . He sh

outed ," shiro ...."

Shiro stop and see back . He run fast towards Raj. Raj sit and hug him .....he crys a lot

The girl said ," shiro ... Don't do like this with any one.....I am so sorry.....he always do like that ......his name is not shiro .....he is my Henry..." He geT Angry and Said," you theif...you like ....he i

s my shiro.......i search him from 5 years ...... You theif you lier ....why you do this ....." She said ," ohh just shut up.......

He is my dog ....and I am not a theif ....I am the shiro owner who give hi

m second life ....one day ambulance

don't see him. and have accident of him ..... I gave him life ......" He think about that accident...

He hug her and said ," thank you so much to save him....." She said," you are very .....i don't understand you....."

He said ," can I take shiro ..." She said ," no....i can't give you my Henry to you...." He said ," i give you a lot of money," she said ," you ney

Δ• sometimes it is better to live alone

Because it gives you sometime to be know who are u.....

Introduction

The purpose of this research which took place in a "paperless classroom" school was to examine the students' reading and writing preferences in various contexts. A questionnaire was distributed among all the students. The results pointed out that students prefer to read short texts and textbooks from computer screens but they prefer to read longer stories from printed books. Students prefer writing on the computer in cases of writing essays, homework and graphs. However, they prefer handwriting on paper, in cases of free drawing, illustrations and solving questions in math. Boys prefer using computers for reading and writing more than girls, and students that have learning difficulties prefer reading and writing from paper more than regular students. These findings indicate that there are differences in the preferences of students.

Life of a girl...

The story starts from girl house . She is an Indian girl . When she was 10 . She is very kindness girl. She always

Think about others. She is from middle class family

but happy family . All things goes

Properly but one day her father comes and she saw taht her father drinked first time . The time goes continuously her father always drink ed at night with his friends and comes home late.

She has 2 sister s and 2 brother. Her big brother is disable. She born after 2sister and small brother is after her . Her name is Rani .

After 6 years later

Her family condition is now.......

Her father beats her mother at night. Karma said " if a man expects a woman to be an angel in his life. Firstly create heaven for her . Angels don't live in hell.

But in her life .

In school she always smile in front of her friends but inside she lost in her problems.

She has a best friend. Her best friend said always to her that say everyone that you are 4 brother and sister her best friend feel guilty because her best friend is having a disable brother.

When she is in 9 class. They divide the class in 9A and 9B . She is in 9B and her best friend is in 9 B .

Her life is changed now.......

She meet a lot of friends who take care of her. One boy who always flirt with girls

And he also flirt with her. One day she bunk the class. She studying

But also live and enjoy the life with that bastard friends . Also her class teacher doudt that a boy is her boyfriend but she didn't know that he is only Rani's friend.

But now in her family they not fear with her father. One day at night her father comes late at home . And her father drinked a lot that's why he can't ride thd bike and slipped in the seaver . Some boys going from that way so they help of her father

They bring him to his home. The grandfather angry too much . Her father comes inside the house. Her grandfather said to them thanks a lot. The boys goes from there. Her grandfather comes inside the house and take slipper and beats in her father cheeks .

Rani's mother stop to her grandfather . Her grandfather also abusing to her father a lot. She said nothing. She puts all talks in her heart .

When she was 15years old......

In summer vacation she go in her village with her 1sister and grandfather, grandmother. A boy in the village who loves her . He proposed to her and she don't having any feelings for him but she asked to her sister;"if I said to him no ...so what happened..."his sister said;" he don't feel good and get to much sad...."

Then she said,"if I said yes to him then ...."his sister said,"he is too happy..." She don't take care of her feelings. She said yes to him and he do from Village to his town and she also go her town

The summer vacation is over.

Her sister search his I'd and she talk to him in I'd . After few days she see that he always come online but he didn't reply and response to her. He always give late reply to her . She breakup with him by her heart. And she never talk to him .

The flirty boy alway said to her i love you but she ignore him .

In class 9 she met a new girl who live in same place. She made her friend and her friend is having a boyfriend . We all know that in adult age we having a attachment to any person .

She and her friend go to in her boyfriend place to buy milk. Her boyfriend having many friends and she also talkna lot with that boy . She thinks that she loved with him

But she didn't know that this feeling is called attachment. Then she comes in relation.

1month later she knew that this is only an attachment because her sister

also tell her attachment with a boy that she gave the name of love . So that's why she also breakup with him.

In class 10th now her real love story begin from here .....

The flirty boy always said her i love you but she didn't response to him . He always

come near to her and sit with her . All class teasing to them .

He also hold her hand .

But now the feeling comes for flirty boy by her. When she saw him and he came closer to her the heart beat continuously. She don't know what the feeling comes in her heart when she saw her. But one day that boy made a girlfriend who study in her class . She didn't show jealousy in face but she jealous . They sit together and hold each other hands .

But one day she talk the boy in WhatsApp. They talk a lot . He said

to her can u come in relationship with me .

She said but you are in relationship .

He said but I love you not her . Then a message comes to her from her friend

She see that her friend write s that Rani, please said yes to him ..he really loved you....

Her friend continuously message to her and he also .

Then she said yes to her .

They got too much happy ,he call to her and they talk too much.

She thinks that he only loved her .

He said to her when she breakup with me then I come with u..

She said ok.

After 2-3 days he didn't break up with her . He said that she won't break up with me

She said it's ok I move back and I didn't come in the middle of you and her . He said sorry'.....

She breaks a lot with her family issues and one more breaks her heart .

After 2-3 month later ...

He and she got break up. He said that she too much jealous when I sit and talk with any girl .

Then he asked to her can u come in relationship with me. She said no and I didn't come in relationship with any one now. There friendship is like that some days thay talk a lot and somedays they act like that they didn't know each other . They are like stranger.

The COVID -19 comes in India. The lockdown is start and their talks is stopped.

After 8 months later the schools are opens . They go to school.

Rani and he didn't talk to each other but after some time they talk a lot . But

again COVID comes so lock down is start.

In lockdown her family condition.....

Her father drink a lot . Her disable brother got fever. His health is not well . His body is like skull

The grand father, father takes care of the brother a lot but medicine didn't work.

In 8 June 2021 morning...

Her brother Died in front of all family members . Now she didn't believe in god . For *her*

The god is died because she pray for her brother a lot . But the god didn't listen her prey

But one day at evening the TV opens the "Mahabharata " comes . She didn't want to see but her soul

Push her to see Mahabharata . She see that Krishna said to Arjun ," no one can live permanently in world □ one day that live this world . This is the rule of the world ."

When she listens that thing. She thinks a lot . She also think at night. Then she realised that death is the bitter truth o f this world. Now

She believes in kanhaji a lot .

After some days her father drinked. In the school the fees is pending a lot of her and her brother and sister. The school stuff said to them always that submit your fees but they don't have money.

One day her father is having a accident. Her father hurt in his mouth but hurt too much.

Her father take to much loan from many people the people comesIn her home to take money.

After few months later her father is very sick her mother take too loan for her father

Now she knew that a wife can bring back her husband's life even from the mouth of death ..... Her mother takes care a lot of her father and she also . Her father get well.

After few months later the school is open. Her big sister vis in the college and her 2sister having board exam so her fees is submit by taking loan . Rani is not good at study . She like to write story , k drama made paintings,anime . She is in class 11 and she failed in 1 subject so she gave retest and pass the class . Now she is in class 12. She just wants to do something for her family. Too many times her father break her heart because he said that he didn't trust in her , you can't do anything in your life bla bla.....

Now she live the life with her break heart.....

This is the story of Rani....

Life quotes

Δ• when the darkness knock the door so the happiness is hide somewhere and we want to find our happiness in the darkness their is a hope with us and that hope is kanhaji.....

Δ• Women are better at love than men

That's why god made the mother.......

Δ• Live your life With your own method not others methods...

Δ• Little by little , day by day what is meant by you it will find a way.....

Δ• whatever happened, happened for good, whatever is happening, happening is good , whatever will happens,

Will also happens the good

Δ• if you don't fight for what you want Don't cry for what you lost....

Δ• love is most beautiful thing in the world that can't be seen, can't be touched, it can only be

Felt in the heart....

Δ•if you do not get your love than definitely give love to those

Who love you .....

Δ• funny have some times a person who is thousand of miles away from you can make

you feel good than people right next to you.......

Δ• And a solution to all your problems is Krishna ....

Δ• seeing some one's pain if you also have pain then understand that Krishna

Is seated in your soul......

Δ• love is that condition in which happiness of another person is essential to your

One.......

Δ• some times your heart needs more time to accept

What your mind already knows......

Δ• He said, where there is love , there is my grace...."

Krishna

Δ• To love without condition, to talk without intention,

To give reason and to give without expectation that's the spirit of soul......

Δ• how many obstacles were seen in love ,

Still saw Radha with Krishna.....

Δ• Krishna's love is like an ocean you can see it's beginning but the beautiful thing is that

You can't see it's end......

Δ• if you think he is not answering your prayers.

Just remember , he feels your pain ......

Δ• Krishna knows what you want and

He will give you what's best for you.......

Δ• nothing is constant in this world every grief and sorrow

Comes to teach the lesson of life ....

Δ• It is better to live your own destiny

Imperfectly than

To live imitation of some body

else'slife with perfection............

Δ• if you want to know what will happen to you in the future look

At what your mind is doing now

KARMA......

Δ• you learn more from failure than from success

Don't let it stop you failure builds

Character.........

Δ• two things I'll forever be sure of the sun will always fall for

Moon and I will always fall for you

Krishna..........

Δ• keep Krishna in the centre of your life and do everything for him

This is real dharma.......

Δ• if you fail to achieve your goal Change the strategy!!!

Not the goal.......

Δ• other may arise doudts over your ability and effort but if you do

Not believe in your self,

This is the same confessions of your failure.........

Δ•earn two friends in your life

One like Krishna who will not fight but will make sure you win......

And another like Karna who will fight for you even when you are wrong.........

Δ• never touch a women ego !!!

One day she may burst

Life a volcano.........

Δ• what parents do for us

And what they get in return......

Δ• Freedom comes with sacrifice....

Δ• never underestimate the importance of small steps

Δ• one day you fell Life is difficult,

But then the results can be very great ....

Δ• always remember that you are an influence

In some body life.....

Δ• Don't be sad if someone reject you

People usually reject expensive things and go for cheaper ones......

Δ• love is based on respect not

Face cut and body shapes........

Δ• sometimes you don't even realise what god

is doing for you.........

Δ• only mother can sacrifice and smile both at same time......

Δ• when you approach with love

Krishna reciprocate with love.......

Δ• the body has many needs

But the soul has only one to be with Krishna.........

Δ• Krishna is real soulmate of every soul.........

Δ• everyone talks about a mother's love

But never see a father's sacrifice........

Δ• use the pain as fuel and keep going.......

Δ• some people sell happiness while

They don't taste any for it.........

Δ• before you build for others

Build your own castle first.......

Δ• a good book can change your life........

Δ• never wish life were easier,

Wish that you were better.........

Δ• Happiness is a state of mind........

Δ• LIFE is not same for everyone.......

Δ• no one is coming to save you ,

Your life is 100% your responsibility......

Δ• when love is true ,

Then even deadlist become loveliest........

Δ•How you see the world depends on how you look...........

Δ• only true friend stab you in front..........

Δ• nowadays people are forced to wear a fake smile...........

Δ• stop creating problems that aren't even there ....

Δ• Never ever depends on anyone if they leave you will get broken severely.........

Δ• nobody on earth can ever love you more than your parents.......

Δ• don't expect victory without a fight ....

Δ• the best way to help yourself is to help someone else...........

¶• don't judge others you are not perfect..........

Δ• some people poor by money but rich by heart'.........

Δ• believe in yourself........

Δ• when you overthink everything you end up hurting yourself.......

Δ• life is like a boomerang you get back what you give.......

Δ• we meet everyone for a reason either they are a blessing or a lesson.......

Δ• spirituality is not about for god truth or the ultimate,

But about learning to just look.......

Δ• Love is that condition in which the happiness of another person is essential to your own ......

Δ• the closer i I get the more I see from far I am.........

Δ• patience is when you're supposed to be mad but you choose to understand........

Δ• TO those who have conquered themselves,

The will is a friend. But it is the enemy of those who have not found the self within them........

Δ• Krishna is the most beautiful name in the world.......

Δ• darkness Can't drive out darkness only light and do that hate can't drive it

hate only love can do that.......

Δ• when you turn your worry into worship

Krishna will true your battles into blessing......

Δ• the struggle in life is not time management it's priority management.......

Δ• why do you worry without cause?

Whom do you fear without reason?

Who can kill you?

The soul is neither born nor does it die ....

Δ• we come in this world empty handed........

Δ• the world is perishable and whenever comes to this world surely has to go one day

Δ• truly can never be destroyed,

One should not be afraid of doing good.......

Δ• what have you lost that you cry for ?

What did you bring that you have lost ?

What did you create that was destroyed?

What you have taken that has been from here ?

What you gave has been given here?

Δ• what belongs to you today belonged to someone else's yesterday and

Will be someone else's tomorrow ....

Δ• change is the law of universe ....

Δ• Radha Krishna love is very precious

Explain to the whole world the value of love ....

Δ• if you like someone you will hold him

And if you love him you will free him ....

Δ• do everything you have to do

But not with ego not with lust not with envy

But with love compassion humility and devotion........

Δ• it is better than beating the head at the door is fate

Creating a storm of deeds

The door will open automatically

Δ• 3 reason why you should smile every day

God loves you

God listen you

God always be with you

Δ• life is not qualified by fluent English branded clothes or a rich lifestyle

It is measured by the no. Of faces who smile when they hear your name......

Δ• if you don't have the right word for a situation then just smile

The can get entangled but smile always work........

Δ• the colour blue represent his infinite force . He is bluish because he is infinite, cosmie and

Immeasurable like the sky which end cant be discovered.......

Δ• I have purpose for your pain

A reason for your struggle and

A reward for your faithfulness

Trust me and Don't give up

Δ• Change is the law of the world

In a moment you become the owner of millions

And in other you become penniless......

Δ• have faith in God's grace

There wherever you go, you will achieve victory .....

Δ• stop counting two things in your life

Your own sorrow and other happiness....

Δ•The relationship of love can broken by saying a lie

But the relationship of heart can never be broken...

Δ• cheating is a choice,

Not a mistake...

Loyalty is a responsibility not a choice

Δ• waiting is a sign of true love and patience

Anyone can say I love you but not everyone can wait and prove it true's....

Δ• you can become very dangerous when you' ll learn how to control your feelings and emotions. ....

Δ• people make the mistake of choosing the wrong person first and when the right person arrives they just stop trusting people ....

Δ• trust his words

Trust his decision

Trust his vision

Trust his deeds

Trust kanhaji once, he entrust himself forever.....

Δ• smiling has always been easier than explaining why you are sad

Δ• god end's anything on a negative

God always ends in positive....

Δ• I am true believer in karma

You get what you give whether it is good or bad ...

Δ• the world gonna judge you no matter what you do so live the life the way you want to...

Δ• if you focus on hurts you will continue to suffer

If you focus on the lesson you will continue to grow....

Δ• the only women who understands me is my mom.....

Δ• life is a book everyday a new page every month is a new chapter and every year is a new series......

Δ• death is not the greatest loss in life

The greatest loss is what dies inside us while we live

Δ• death is bitter truth of life

Δ• don't tell your secret to anyone your today's bestie is your tommorrow is worst enemy....

Δ• don't be too happy when people say they love you and care you

The real question is until when!

Because just like seasons people change

Δ• if you' ll prioritize chanting

Krishna will prioritize you

Δ• if it's true

It will stay

Δ• Krishna is not punishing you. He is preparing you .

Trust his plans not your pain

Δ• and then there's some conversations that you just save for the god

It's because only god provide the kind of comfort that humans cannot

Δ• These black clouds in the sky reminds me of my fears and

I love it when it rains on now well it hide my tears

Δ• fear is not an obstacles

It's an illusion because fear is only made by you

Δ• if you want to be strong learn to fight alone

The second story is of a animal or a boy .....

The story starts from the boy house. The boy name is Raj.

He sleep in his room and a box open and a dog come out of that box and tried to pick him up by licking

His mouth. He wakes up and brushes his tooth . His mother call him ," Raj come on for breakfast..." Raj said," ya.. I am coming". He wears his school dress and come to kitchen for breakfast. He say ," good morning..mom" and sit in his seat and doing breakfast. His father comes and sit for breakfast. Raj said," good morning....papa

His father said," good morning......I want to ask you that you didn't take that dog again. " Raj said," no ...no..."

His father said," don't tell a lie if you bring that dirty dog so it is my last warning get out that dirty dog...." Raj said," please papa I can't do this with shiro" his father said," if you can't do this so I can "

Raj caught his father legs and requested from him .but he didn't listen to him

go in his room. The shiro sleep in his bed . He wake Up and licking him

but he is in so anger he catch him so badly and throw him out from the house . Shiro get hurt too much

His father warn to everyone....and go to office.

Raj crying in his room. Raj's mother said to her," mummy Mahesh...." Her mother said," i know all things"

Then she go in Raj room . He is crying their. She put hand on his head . She strocked his head . She said," i know my son that why are you crying.... You think about shiro .." her grandma support him and give love to him.....

Then he go to school. He meet with his friends who know all things about his family....When school is over

Raj go in ground to meet shiro . He bandaged him and give him food . And said ," their is no one who understands me accept you...."

At night the rain come suddenly . He think about shiro

So he go IN ground shiro is wet in rain he made a house for shiro.

And give him food...

Then he go to house.....

Next morning he is I'll and he can't go to school ... Her grandma come and said," don't worry i give food to shiro ....ok...""

He is too happy and hug grandma..... laugh

Two days later.....

Her Grandma have a heart attack ..... suddenly...they admitted her grandma

But her grandma has died he cry too much ....

5 YRs later

HE Made a big business man . But shiro has get lost somewhere.

He search him every where but he didn't meet him.....

But suddenly one day

In night time he see that a girl who is having shiro . He sh

outed ," shiro ...."

Shiro stop and see back . He run fast towards Raj. Raj sit and hug him .....he crys a lot

The girl said ," shiro ... Don't do like this with any one.....I am so sorry.....he always do like that ......his name is not shiro .....he is my Henry..." He geT Angry and Said," you theif...you like ....he i s my shiro.......i search him from 5 years ...... You theif you lier ....why you do this ....." She said ," ohh just shut up.......

He is my dog ....and I am not a theif ....I am the shiro owner who give hi

m second life ....one day ambulance

don't see him. and have accident of him ..... I gave him life ......" He think about that accident...

He hug her and said ," thank you so much to save him....." She said," you are very .....i don't understand you....."

He said ," can I take shiro ..." She said ," no....i can't give you my Henry to you...." He said ," i give you a lot of money," she said ," you ney

Δ• sometimes it is better to live alone

Because it gives you sometime to be know who are u.....

www.ingramcontent.com/pod-product-compliance
Lightning Source LLC
LaVergne TN
LVHW050421160726
843469LV00041B/1175